Living in A Country Influenced By

Living in A Country Influenced By Hate

Written by author

Marlon Reid

A

Marlon Reid Productions

Your Efforts Need to Be Bigger Than Your Dreams

Living in A Country Influenced By
Hate
Dear America

This letter is for you and your forefathers who wrote the constitution back in 1887 over three centuries ago. These laws are affecting one race because of the color of our skin which you named it the color, black, brown, and African American. They took it upon themselves and said we are not living by GOD ten commandments we are writing our own laws to live by. A white man founded this country so white men will design how people will live in this country. First and foremost, **GOD** created this land the white man did not find this country first people were already living here.

When the forefathers wrote the constitution, they did not include African American to be a part of it that is why in 2020 our rights are being violated. They think the second Amendment gives them the right to kill black people (*I was afraid for my life*) are the famous words they love using. White people use this in court after killing one of us and the jury find them innocent when GOD said thy should not kill.

Let me tell you something Don King said it best only in America yes, I am talking about the land of the free and the home of the brave. I am talking about where a white boy can go inside a church doing

Living in A Country Influenced By Hate

bible study and PRAYER shoot the church up killing nine African American and leave out in handcuffs.

In other news a crooked white cop pulls a black couple over for a routine stop kills the black UNARMED man in front of his family. This is crazy the color of your skin can determine if you are handcuffed or get a body bag. From what I seen this been happening my whole entire life blacks get a body bag. You never hear a white man getting shot by a black cop or by a white cop you always hear we have the suspect in custody.

Dear America, this the type of hatred this country has for people like me who skin is a little darker than the other races. America you lie to us about the statue of liberty and what she supposed to represent. Freedom of the slaves are why the chain are still in front of her right feet yet instead they flipped it to use it for a peace treaty between France and the United States for immigrants. African Americans we are immigrants this is not our country we were brought here?

Sometimes I sit back and wonder how my ancestors went from being KINGS & QUEENS to slaves and maids to walking and marching with Dr. King and standing strong with Malcolm x.

The speech we shall overcome someday was powerful as a speech or a preach could be

Living in A Country Influenced By Hate

delivered and what the white America do killed one of our greatest leaders. All because he wanted unity amongst us all as one Nation Under GOD, they also could've stopped Malcolm X from being murdered they knew and they let it happen because to them just one more of us out the way. America been treating us unfairly since they brought us to this country look at Ms. Rosa parks, she just got tired of sitting on the back of the bus look what they done locked her up because she refused. In the 60s, we could not even use the same bathroom or drink from the same water fountain as white people did.

Yet instead they still call this country the land of the free, so you are telling me that was not violating our constitutional rights I guess not because they wrote them. Up until this day what they wrote for all human's races to live by they do not honor it not towards black people.

Dear America, how could you say hate have no home here when you have hatred groups like white supremacy, KKK and many others hate groups. Confederate flags, statues, around the south and you know what they represent? but instead America kept those racists symbol hanging high for people to see them. Let me correct that statement for BLACK people to be reminded what they kind did to our ancestors. Try to look at this from a black

Living in A Country Influenced By Hate

person point of view this how we see this we see it as devastation, destruction, evil, one race wants to be superior.

Then came the 70s and 80s where you did these experiments on us with drugs and building tall projects because that is just what that was a project. To keep us contained to keep us in poor living conditions to find a way to fill up your prison system to try and keep us from being SUCCESSFUL.

America did just that when they put the guns and crack into our communities in the late 70s and early 80s it was like putting a lab rat in a cage doing experiments and watching the outcome.

We did not put these things in our communities see dear America you knew what type of effects and outcome this would have but once again you did not care.

Dear America, you choose green over black matter of fact you choose green over every color and over every race we just get it worse than everybody else. You knew the devastation and destruction drugs, money, and guns would bring into a poor community. You kept us in bondage and chains for years and you do not want me to be mad? I do not suppose too feel any kind of hate toward you. The

Living in A Country Influenced By Hate

bible tells us Love your neighbors as you love yourself Matthews 22:39 why is that so hard for you to do dear America.

I tell you why because this country is full of hate and full of Disgrace this starts inside of someone household you are not born with hate you are born into hate.

Dear America, I am a black man living in this country we call the home of the brave and the land of the free but from what I seen and experience this country is far from that. Yes, America you gave me opportunity, but my opportunities lacks the same opportunities that are given to a white man. Our schools are different our education is different our neighborhoods are different all because the color of our skin is different. You build our communities close and bunched up together in the inner cities, but you build the white community space out wide in the suburban areas. You try to make everything different between us but when GOD created us the only thing, he made different between us are men and women but, GOD created us all EQUAL. all men have the same body parts and all women have the same body parts two eyes, two ears, two arms and hands and two legs with two feet. Tell me dear America why do the white race think they are more superior if we were created in his Image who created us EQUAL.

Living in A Country Influenced By Hate

Sometimes I sit back and think what if GOD Created us all with one color what if that color was all brown skinned how would the world be would it be racism would it be black on black crime. Would cops still be killing our kind would there have been slavery these the things that goes through my mind when I see the injustice that we receive as black people. Sometimes I ask GOD why? this is the flesh part of me asking SPIRITUAL I know GOD is in control I know he is the beginning and the end.

Dear America, we as a race are sick and tired of you killing us from back in the days with our Ancestors lecturing and hanging us up until now shooting and choking us. A line that is becoming deadly and famous I cannot breathe is being heard too often in this day and time. We will take to the streets every time you racist bigots kill one of us, we are going to marching and protest and tear down your racist symbols. I do not condone the violence or looting but this seemed to be the only way to get their attention to let them know we are tired. I understand fire cannot be put out with fire but sometimes they make you want to fight them back with fire.

We say no more meaning give us our equal rights as human beings stop separating equal justice stop discriminating the law because our skin color is darker. Stop finding your color Innocent because

Living in A Country Influenced By Hate

they are white stop leaving our families in the courtrooms heartbroken in tears in disbelief because you claimed there was not enough evidence to convince the racism bigot who murdered our Love one.

Dear America we say no more it's time to fight back it's time to stand up we want to stay alive yes, we are going to march like Martin but we are going to come force like Malcolm preach like Martin but push back like Malcolm. Every time you take a black person life from here on out you will feel our present doing sporting events, we will take a knee⬛⬛ and sing BLACK-POWER.

Dear America, we will print your flag black and white see you worrying about a football player disrespecting a flag and a song, but you been disrespecting us as human beings since you brought us over to America. If we do not see the NFL as being racist or standing with them than something is wrong with our eyes, they fired and black balled a black man because he took a knee doing a song for JUSTICE rights. Yes, a knee doing a song, but the punk Police can take a knee on a black man neck killing him and it take days before you arrest him.

See Kaepernick stood for something more than just a football player more than being a quarterback

Living in A Country Influenced By Hate

more than being a team player his cause stood for a whole entire race. His causes for equal rights and justice shook up a whole nation effected a whole entire country gave people mixed emotions mixed feelings. At one-point Kaepernick had white football owners' coaches and players locking arms and kneeling embracing the moment. See this thing was deep until the President flipped it and made about, them disrespecting the troops who fought and die for this country. You must remember blacks and Puerto Rican, Mexicans, many others die for this country Drew breeds not just your grandfather. You are entitled to your opinion I just hope you see what the cause really stand for injustice is what we been receiving as a race since day one. Dear America, you gave us one win in the O.J Simpson case and we been losing ever since that day.

Dear America, I would like to thank every race from man, women, and children who are standing with us doing this time fighting for justice in the Gorge Floyd case. This is what we needed everyone to come together as a nation the world got involved different countries standing up and walking the walk we need for justice for Brianna Taylor.

See dear America we are not the only ones tired of your selfish disgraceful ways everybody is tired of

Living in A Country Influenced By Hate

the hate that live here the hate you keep allowing to get away with injustice.

For real that racist you have in the white house is the biggest one of them all the things you allowed him to get away with as a President a man a father as a husband is despicable. He is so horrible, but this is what America stand on green $$$$$ and the white race wants to be in control talking about let us make America great again. The same words came out the mouth of the confederations who wrote the constitution.

2016-2020 have been by far the worst four years I have ever seen in the White House I am 44yrs old if you are older you may see different. Therefore, we must get out and vote let us take this same energy we have for protesting take it to the poles. Come November use the mailbox if we must mail them in. I just hope they do not rob Biden the same way as they did Hillary back in 2016 because if so, he will start a war before he leaves office in 2024.

The devastation he will bring will leave a horrific impact on the world not just in the United States, all of this crazy and wild stuff that are happening is a distraction for him and his team to do any and everything to win this November election. Sometimes America will make you think your vote doesn't count because look at what happened in

Living in A Country Influenced By Hate

the 2016 election good people don't let 2016 election discourage you get out and vote this is what they want us to be discouraged. This is the time to be more encourage because once again this election is about change history in the making the first black women to be a running mate for vice president.

This president will be one to remember because of his Ignorance and arrogant ways he did just about anything he wanted and got away with it. This president gets on TV, Twitter and says anything he wants to and gets away with it regardless who is offended.

Even other countries ask Americans how you let this happen all we can tell them; it was out of our hands we voted.

If this is making America great again, I know I do not want any parts of this in my eyes making America great is equal JUSTICE. Making America great is building more shelter for the homeless with better programs on living and managing your financial stop closing schools in the black, Latino and Mexican communities. Start funding money in the low-income areas fix up the community's centers get back to after-school's program.

Dear America, you are still claiming hate have no home here when over the past few months people were founded hanging from a tree in all different states right next to those racist towns. Reports said these people committed suicide by hanging their selves now that just do not sound right to me. A black man hanging himself in this day and time knowing what our ancestors went through just me but, I strongly believe they were murder lynch by a group of hateful people like Don King said only in America.

As I end this chapter, I PRAY that you understand where I am coming from what type of mindset, I am in and where my heart is at. I am not going to lie to you my heart is half anger and the other half is full of joy.

My rage for revenge is growing because I know at any given time when I walk out of my door that could be the last time my family sees me. I know my life could be taken by the hands of a crooked officers or a racist bigot a drunk driver or even my own kind through black on black crime. So, as you see our odds is outnumber in this country by an exceptionally large margin yes, I feel like when I leave out my house I need to be strapped with a gun.

The consequences that gun holds for me if I get pulled over by the police it is life or death

Living in A Country Influenced By Hate

everything, I worked so hard to get will be gone in a blank of an eye. If the police see the gun they may say they fear for their life and open up fire striking and killing me or take me to jail and when come trial they find me guilty on possession of a deadly weapon because of my past convictions and get 20 years. Now do you understand the rage part of me as a black man living in America with the odds stacked against me because to them, I am still a criminal with a record. It does not matter if I have not been in trouble the last 15 years a criminal is a criminal to them. It does not matter if I became a deacon it does not matter if I am a husband or a father or an Inspirational figure an author with four inspiring books as a black man that means nothing to them. I am talking about them crooked cops they will still kill me I am talking about black on black crime they will kill me especially if I cannot carry a gun to fire back. I am talking about America who will convince me if they catch me carrying one to protect myself and my family.

The black man has a lot of weight on his shoulder he must watch his self from every angle in front of him behind him and to the left and right of him. A black man must watch out for crooked cops' racist white people and most of all the ones who look just like him.

Living in A Country Influenced By Hate

Let me not forget my black and beautiful sisters our black queens our black mothers our black women. Who are the wives, the girlfriends, the sisters, the baby mothers, the aunts the nieces, the daughters and finally our mothers to the black men who are being murdered? Your actions are not just affecting the black man you are killing but it is affecting his whole entire family.

Dear America, this is so saddened, but you treat animal abusers worse than you treat white cops and white people who kill black people. Look at the Michael Vick situation and look at all the cop's situations I think just one cop is serving time out of the many who are crooked murderers.

Even when someone say something hateful to a gay person you will charge them with terrorists' threats and give them a few years. Let alone if someone kill a gay person you charge them with a hate crime and murder, sentence them to 25yrs to life in prison. When a crooked police officer kills an unarmed black man or women it is never enough inclusive evidence to convince or to be found guilty. The same way when a white person or any other race kills a black person there's never enough evidence look at George Zimmerman free as of right now.

Living in A Country Influenced By Hate

I will not lie when Zimmerman verdict came back not guilty, I want the black people living in Florida to burn that courthouse down to the ground yes, I did. That is the flesh side of me who wanted revenge who wanted justice who wanted to say forget about peace now we are going to taking our rage out on every white person we see and come across.

The SPIRITUAL side kept me calm and PRAYING for HEALING for STRENGTH for his father, mother, and the rest of his family who would 've not wanted that.

Dear America you have some nerve to even put up a statue like Lincoln's where he is standing up over a black man who looks to be on his knees and Lincoln have his left hand over top of his head. This statue is a disgrace to black people matter of fact that statue represent what Lincoln really was all about. Yes, that is my opinion of Lincoln yes, he signed the freedom for slavery to end and for blacks to be free. We were not, he just signed a piece of paper stating that we were free, but it took at least 2yrs for it to happen. If Lincoln really wanted us to be free Lincoln would have pushed harder, but he did not Lincoln was the president of the United States at the time.

Living in A Country Influenced By Hate

Understand this good people these are just my thoughts and opinions on Lincoln no I do not know him personally but from what I read I just don't believe he was as good as they said he were. If you disagree that is fine with me.

Dear America, the 14th Amendment all persons born or naturalized in the United States and subject to the jurisdiction thereof, are citizens of the United States and of the states wherein they reside. No state shall make or enforce any law which shall abridge the privilege or immunities of citizens of the United States; nor shall any state deprive any person of life, liberty, or property, without due process of law; nor deny to any person within its jurisdiction the equal protection of the laws. This is what you wrote but when it comes to black people equal rights you proceed with the law on the 2nd amendment a right to bear arms ruling in white people favor. After they committed murder, I tell you it's hard living in America an being African American but don't get me wrong I am still grateful to live in America because I know many others countries have way more struggles then America.

Dear America, I am grateful to live here but I am not proud to live here I do realize the opportunity you given me are way better than the opportunity you gave my ancestors. Because of their walks and

Living in A Country Influenced By Hate

marches for freedom there blood their death there fight I know our reasons why we do have opportunities.

I do not hate this country not at all I hate what this country allows whites to do to black people. I do not like how the so call powers to be always turning their heads when it comes to justice for us. Because let us get one thing straight if a black person breaks the law in any way, they will be prosecuted to the full extent except for OJ who beat them I said before we been paying for his not guilty verdict ever since.

I will say this America allowed many black people to do some great things yes, we came along way and we created some of our own great historical times.

From becoming musicians, entrepreneurs, TV and film entertainers, billionaires Minister, and to sit in the high seat at the white house is something extraordinary. I know the goodness that is inside of this country because GOD turned my life around in this same country. I know people outside of my race are tired of seeing injustice being done to us 2020 have been a year America or the world will not forget. A few unjustified police officers killing black people made a change this time around. People took to the streets marching and looting

Living in A Country Influenced By Hate

burning buildings and police cars tearing down racist symbols around the United States. This time different races were attracted by the hate we received from the ones who took a pledge to sever and to protect the citizens. Different races got to see our reality firsthand by being shot with rubber bullets getting tear gas and arrested because they are peacefully protesting.

Thank you for stepping up and stepping in because without you guys help America not going to listen to us but since different races joined the cause now America is listening. Police laws are being changed racist symbols are being taken down the they are starting to realize that the 14 amendment reply to African Americans to.

We still have a lot to fix but 2020 helped to give us a start R.I.P to all who lives was sacrificed.

BLACK IS BEAUTIFUL

Black is beautiful black is love black girls rock black is powerful black do not crack black stand for king and queen brothers and sister's black means culture. To be a black person is to be a strong person when GOD created us GOD gave us different colors as black people. When GOD created our skin color, he gave us brown skin light skinned people a darker skinned black he created us with three different colors out of one-color

Living in A Country Influenced By Hate

black. Look around the world when a different race mixes their skin color with black look how beautiful it looks. Black is positively look at what black have created the Obamas, the Al Sharpton the LeBron James etc. Now when I say create, I know GOD created us lets me clarify the air because I know the top holy people will hold me accountable. To be black is to be great to be black is to be appreciate it what is the old saying once you go black you never go back ask the white women, she will tell you. To be black is to be bold to be black means you must strive a lot hard than the rest. To be black is to be feared black is POWERFUL in every way possible our skin color has so much value to it. We can adapt to any situation they put us in just check our history we fought we battle we PRAYED we walked we fell we got back up and kept going we are survivors. In 2020 we are still battling the odds against us make no mistake we will win.

October 15, 1966 in Oakland CA the Black Panthers started their organization for justice and the rights for African American. Two young men who was tired of police brutality to black people these young men who wanted to stand up for our rights. Look how America flipped it and made them look violent, they hated to see us start a strong movement.

BLACK LIVES MATTER

Living in A Country Influenced By Hate

Is another movement against hateful behavior against racism a fight for peace and justice look how this weak president trump tried to flip this into something else? See black is POWERFUL black is positive black is STRENGTH if black was not all these words, I just mention why do they go out of their way to try and destroy something so great.

To be black is to be something unique being black is something to be proud of because I know when we walk into a room our skin color is important it is very encouraging. We know GOD created us the same way as he created every other race standing in that same room.

To be black is to be able to move a whole culture being black is being able to dictate what their children love to listen to. What they children love to wear how their children like to talk these days.

The sounds people hear from blackness have the whole world dancing and partying and grooving to the beat so I am confused on how they can love our culture but hate our skin color.

Look how black women changed the fashion change how women around the world want their bodies to look like. The thickness of the thighs the roundness of their butts the sexiness of their walk

Living in A Country Influenced By Hate

to the boldest of their mouths. Look how the black women persona are dominating the world. Remember back in the 80s the black women body was concerned fat and out of shape nasty and sloppy. Now her same body shape has different women of many different races getting operations and surgeries to look how **GOD** created hers.

Do you see how powerful our black woman is to this earth today not just about her body I am talking way deeper than that. I am talking about Her brain Opera Winfrey I am talking her about accomplishments Michelle Obama I am talking about her voice Patty Labelle. I am talking about her fights Rosa Louise McCauley Parks I am talking about her beauty Alicia keys.

I am talking about my beautiful wife and my two wonderful daughters I thank GOD for allowing me to wake up to every day to hear their voices and to see them put a big smile on their faces.

Black is the thing to be I use to love hearing my grandparents play Marvin Gaye's music I remember watching TV in the early 80s seeing Sidney Poitier he made black wonderful to watch. Martin Luther King gave us hope Malcolm X gave us strength Run DMC gave us rhythm and style and when 2pac first came out he gave us a voice. President Obama showed us change and Benjamin

Living in A Country Influenced By Hate

Crump gives us justice Michael Jordan made us wanted to become an athlete not just a basketball player. He had black's whites, Puerto Rican, saying I want to be like Mike now tell me BLACK is the thang to be powerful.

I remember in the early 90s watching David Reid train hard every day to reach his gold medal to be able to watch him win the gold medal in the 96 Olympics for boxing let me know dreams do come true for black people.

David Reid accomplishments made me know black is the thang to be even now in 2020 watching a great smart man from my neighborhood become a black entrepreneur building an empire out of real of state gives us hope and inspiration Greg Parker thanks.

This skin color that we are living in as African Americans is nothing more than a BLESSING, I just cannot see it any other way. Yes, our skin color gave us a lot of struggles and I mean a lot but at the same time our skin color brought us so much JOY.

Black people never let nobody tell you that black is not the thang to be see if you are not black you just cannot understand it this it is a black thang. I am not taking anything away from any other race

Living in A Country Influenced By Hate

because I love you all I may not like you but the GOD in me is allowing me to love you.

This chapter here is a celebration to my people from the past my present and to the ones in the future I am letting them know that we are well appreciate it despite what we went through and what we are currently going through. We are standing tall in many categories these words right here are for you my little brothers and sisters your future is bright, and your present is STRONG. Young generation you are the future and because of your past your path on your journey will be that much more noticeable so do not be afraid be encourage. Do not run away from its gratitude towards it because your history his indeed that powerful.

Know this black people we are shining our culture is what many other cultures want to be look at them you will see our culture in their culture.

My people this is our time be all we can be the BLESSING FROM GOD is with us and if GOD is with us no one can be against us. Over the years they tried and tried but we kept getting up we survived so when you read this chapter know you are Loved.

A Message to Good Cops

People always saying all cops are not bad we do have some good cops out here. My question to that where all the good cops are hiding at because we need them more than ever to step up. If you are a good cop and your partner kills an unarmed person and you are standing there, watching and do nothing to stop it than you are a crooked cop as well. Mr. Good cops you took an oath SERVE and protect just like the bad cops did you do everything you can to bring a criminal to justice a drug dealer a rapist a thief a cop killer but not a killer cop.

Oh, I see Good Office we only see you when someone gun down a cop than that is when you step up to the plate. But when a crooked cop kicks in a door and just start shooting and hit an innocent women 8 times no good cop tries to arrest them. I see every cop who came to sever that warrant must be a bad cop no I was not there, but this is how I feel.

Good cops I know this is your job and I know this is how you pay your bills and put food on your table I understand all of that but sometimes doing the right thing is more important than making money. No, I cannot put myself in your shoes because if I am with someone and they kill somebody, and I do not say anything or tried to stop them than I'm accessory to murder I'm just as guilty conspiracy.

That's just how I see you and I know many will disagree I just might lose so friends over this

Living in A Country Influenced By Hate

chapter because I know people that are married to police officers and I know a few myself. The way I feel at this point I really do not care if anyone stop speaking to me over what I am talking about. I just cannot see how the good cops are not in the wrong because when we are marching and protesting for justice. Over a wrongful cop killing a black person you know where the good cops are standing on the other side of the line defending the crooked cops. Shooting rubber bullets at people who are fighting for justice pushing and shooting tear gas at them is that what good cops supposed to do. Oh, I get it once again this is their job to stop protesters not bad cops, I guess that is internal affairs job to do.

I will say this there was a few cops trying to make peace at some of these rallies this time around I know we have to crawl before we walk. I know what them few officers did was a start I, do appreciate them for stepping up because this George Floyd killing was in plain view. It is no way you good cops can look the other way anymore this time we need you just like we need other races we need you on the front line. No more division over color black, white, or blue this is for human rights I am a black man myself taking a chance every time I leave my house, I can get pulled over by a crooked cop.

Living in A Country Influenced By Hate

Good cops if you know your partner is trigger happy towards black men step in and try to stop it before it happens save a life. You could be saving a son a brother an uncle a cousin a father someone husband do you see the chain one person can be link to.

Remember how many people you are link to good cops you would not want a cop killer to leave your family heartbroken.

Please if you are a cop do not feel any Kind of way after reading this try to have an understanding heart an open mind this was not to bash you in anyway. This was to bring awareness to you on how we feel as black people as citizens of the United States when one of you kills our people for nothing. I wrote this chapter to challenge you to uphold the law against crooked cops who are breaking the law. It does not matter if their color is black, white or if they are wearing a blue shirt sever and protect because if not than we put you in the same category as the bad cops.

PRAYER

May GOD protect you as you put on your uniform every single day may GOD give you the knowledge and understanding to do what you were swear in to do. I PRAY over your Family as well IN THE NAME OF JESUS CHRIST AMEN.

Living in A Country Influenced By Hate
A Message to Bad Cops

I am talking directly to you how could you put on your uniform every day you swore you would serve and protect the citizens of the United States. How could you shoot someone in cold blood or choke the life out of them while they are screaming, I cannot breathe? How could you put your uniform back on after you kill an innocent person how could you go home and look your own child in the eyes knowing that you took someone else child's life. How could you look your spouse, your brother your sister your uncle your cousin a friend a co-worker in the eyes after you murdered someone in cold blood. He or she was important to someone they have love Ones just like you have love ones.

CROOKED OFFICE

How could you look at yourself in the mirror and when you look in the mirror what do you see a demonic present because that is what you are a demon. You put that uniform on and feel like you are untouchable you think you can do whatever you want to a black person and get away with it. America been protecting you for far too long America been sweeping your dirt up under the rug for many years. Them so, call good cop is even more crooked than you bad cops what is that

Living in A Country Influenced By Hate

slogan if you see something say something but instead you do nothing.

CROOK OFFICE

I still remember my first encounter with a crooked cop back in 89 I was 13yrs old when I caught my first drug case. Cop jumped out I ran he chase me, and his partner ran me down and hit me with the cop car found the drugs and kept the money now tell me that was not crooked. See us black folks been dealing with the crookedness from way back when they use put white sheets over their whole body and cover their faces riding horses holding up a burning stick calling themselves KKK.

Now they call themselves police officers, judges, prosecutors, jury, and a host of other things but for now we are going to focus on the crooked cops.

CROOKED OFFICE

You know how we can tell they are crooked because since the George Floyd murder live recording. There has been so many incidents and video recording involving crooked cops. Another white cop shooting a black Man in the back in Atlanta killing him could have been avoided justice for Rashard Brooks.

We have lost some many of our people because the opposite race claim that they fear for their lives when they come across an African American. How could this be when we should be the ones in fear because if you let history tell it you been destroying our race for years. You enslave us back in 1619 raped and impregnated our women took our children from us. In the 1920s you burned down our establishments hung us and beaten us. In the 1950s and 60s you sprayed us with water holes made us use separate bathrooms and drink from different water Fountains.

I am confused how are you scared of us when yawl did all of them horrible things to us.

CROOKED OFFICER

When I look at the men and women in blue, I do not know who to trust when you pull me over, I do not know if I am getting a violation ticket or a Death certificate. This is sad all because of my skin color now you tell me why I suppose to trust you, now you tell me how I can separate the good cops from the bad cops. Tell me do it says good cop on their badge or on their uniform somewhere, how do you know when you are dealing with a good cop because you know when you are dealing with a crooked cop. I guess if you walk away with your life after a confrontation you are dealing with a good cop. Well I am going to end this like I pray the next time a situation comes up in any event you officers realize this is someone life in your hands.

Once a criminal always a criminal in their eyes

This statement right that is so true once you become a number in the system your number is forever. Yes, that goes for all Americans no matter what color you are, but my issue is if you are African American the law pushes that law against us just a little bit harder. We already have a strike against us because of our skin color now you add a criminal record on your jacket it makes getting a good job that more impossible. No, I am not saying it is not possible because I am living proof with a darker skin color and a criminal record you can adjust to living in this society in a positive way.

So, what if you made some mistakes in your lifetime don't let that stop you from doing the right thing, see they designed it that way so you can make the same mistakes once again. It is a Revolving door to Keep us trapped and to keep 80 percent of our children away from their fathers. To have 80 percent of our black women raising their children as a single parent. Do you know how much pressure this puts on a mother who must do it all alone? Do not become a statistic become a suggestion.

Living in A Country Influenced By Hate

To all of our children no matter what color your skin is please understand once you become a number in the system you make your life that much harder do the right thing and say no to drugs on all levels.

Encouraging Words

Everything you need to succeed is already in you just push a little harder.

Never be afraid to ask for HELP.

It is ok to get it wrong a few times that will only makes you want to get it right even more.

Expect someone to tell you NO sometimes

Living in A Country Influenced By Hate
Do not get frustrated learned to have patience with time.

Everything starts with you.

Men

We are living in a time where the presence of men lacks at an all-time high the lack of leadership in the household, inside the schools, and inside churches and other religious ministries. GOD created us to lead the way to be the head and not the tail to be a king to be a Priest to be a Husband a father somewhere down the line we lost hope. Do not get me wrong there are many men around the world representing these titles as GOD needs us to do, I am not talking about all men, but I am talking about men as a collective.

The structural of family is out of order and has been out of order for a longtime our women the mothers of the earth and mothers of the household are left alone to be both parents.

Men, Father's, husbands, Brothers, uncles, sons something must give, and it must give right now we are losing the battle. Fathers are being separated from their SONS and our sons are left to fill in the

Living in A Country Influenced By Hate

void through the streets the same way as his father the chains never being broken the chains only grows with each generation.

How can we as a whole fix this problem that has been lingering for years do, we start with the youth catch them while they are still growing up. Do we start with the men who are stuck in their ways?

There is a book out call Transforming the minds of men written by Bishop Gilbert Coleman what a great book I believe every young boy teenager and man need to have this book. Just like the title describe transforming the mind is where we will need to start at. First thing we will need to do is get their attention second, we need to convince them to listen to what we have to say and third show them better than we can tell them.

As of right now the culture have our children going in the wrong direction and the culture are getting rich from it. While our sons are either getting kill or going to jail and our daughters are becoming strippers and getting into the porn business. You can get mad at me all you want I am not judging I am just saying it is a much better way to live life.

Yes, it is just entertainment, but that entertainment is becoming most people reality the hardest part about change is change.

Living in A Country Influenced By Hate

Men we have A lot of work on our hands and it is not getting any easier in fact it is only getting harder by the day. This **BLACK ON BLACK CRIME** is out of control the value of black's lives means nothing to the black people who are pulling the trigger. We must march in the streets and stand on these corners where all the violence is happening at. No more procrastinating the time is now right now

Black people matter of fact all people we need your same energy your same ambition your same motivation you gave towards the racist protesting. I think it is time for another million-man march rally throughout the streets of America and across the world.

No, we cannot do this alone yes, we need our beautiful women standing with us walking with us you make us that much stronger. I am calling on all the strong WOMAN group out here around the world who are making a positive impact.

I Have learned something along time ago simple math two is stronger than one that is why *JESUS* always sent two disciples to handle a mission so that one can watch over the other. My point is yes, we need our ladies by our sides to help us brainstorm, to help us march, to help us claim VICTORY to help us lead the way.

The less men on the streets the less father figures are in the homes the less father figure the more attractive to negatively the more negatively the lesser chance for successful opportunities.

 The cycle just keeps going and growing leaving a bad reflection on us as men once again I will say not by Individual but by a whole. The blame for this outcome is not men alone a lot of other things played apart like music, fashion, popularity, and this slogan right here *(KEEPING IT REAL)*

Sometimes I sit back alone in my bedroom with the lights off and begin thinking to myself did I help do this when I was younger. Did I wait too late to join in on the rally against violence is this fight far too gone as a man trying to do right do my presence even matter to these young people. What more can I do? Maybe I am asking myself the wrong question maybe I should be telling myself you need to do more. Men I put this on our shoulders because we supposed to be the protectors but 65% of us are pulling the trigger making us out to be the predators. I do believe we will and shall overcome as a great man once said Mr. Dr Martin Luther King

Living in A Country Influenced By
Hate

Jr. With GOD on our side and we are united we have the upper hand VICTORY is ours.

To those that is out here fighting the fight every single day your efforts are well appreciate your passion for peace is so encouraging continue to do the will of **GOD** and the reward will be extremely rewarding. Love, Peace and Strength in **JESUS** name **AMEN.** Thank you To All the Good Men, Women

MOTIVATION POEM

⏹⏹Black Is Power Poem⏹⏹

Black is power

Long as I can remember us blacks Living here, we have always been fighting for power.

America is handing Africa America's their death sentence every hour on the hour.

Because the white supremacy thinks the color of black skin looks sour.

When GOD created our darker skin color GOD created it with such power.

He told us we are a part of this nation yes, it is ours.

They hate it and try to destroy us like Ben Laden did the twins towers.

Living in A Country Influenced By Hate

Like the KKK did when they burned down the black wall streets because it was ours.

Black schools' black hospitals black banks equal up to black power

They put white sheets over their white faces I call them white cowards

Equal rights are our freedom to my people

BLACK POWER, BLACK POWER, BLACK POWER

Equal Rights

The equal rights amendment is a proposed amendment to the United States constitution designed to guarantee equal legal right for all-American citizens No matter race or sex.

Equal

Being the same in quantity, sizes, degree, or value.

Equal

Living in A Country Influenced By Hate

The BIBLE says GOD created man in his own image, in the image of GOD he created him; Male and female he created them.

Equal

There you have its America a few meanings to the word equal and what the word equal stands for.

One Nation Under GOD

When I hear the saying one nation under GOD to me this means all together, a strong force, we the people are one. Somewhere along ago this statement was broken and the bond as one faded away. We can argue and say it was because of religion, skin color, money or who is the more dominant human man or women. I do not know the answer to this frustrated question who do? What I do know there is no room for separation we the people have to stand as one. Will it ever get back to being one nation under GOD in my opinion I truly doubt it not because I lack in faith but, because my faith in people is where I lack at. Sometimes I sit back and daydream about how the world would be if we the people were all on the

Living in A Country Influenced By Hate

same page SPIRITUAL, Physically, financially, mentally.

Would the world be a more peaceful place to live in would the people believe more in GOD and less of the world? Would we be able to live as brothers and sisters would the world be crimeless free?

Once again who knows?

My imagination is what keeps me going something I imagine walking with JESUS when he was here in the flesh. I can only imagine how that experience was, they were **BLESS** to see and hear and feel our **KING** in the flesh.

 I will save my imagination for my fifth book let me get back to this book and topic.

One Nation Under GOD

I remember in elementary school the teachers would have us practice and learn this I pledge allegiance to the flag of the United States of America and to the republic which it stand one nation under God individual with liberty and justice for all.

Written back in 1892 without the under GOD in it 1923 it was changed from to my flag to the flag and last in 1954 Under GOD was added.

Living in A Country Influenced By Hate

My reason for bringing this up is because as a kid I really fed into one nation under GOD thinking we all were equal. Did not understand at that time why I seen white people doing the things they did to black people.

One Nation Under GOD Authority

Dear Brothers and Sisters as the late great Apostle Paul have called us in the past, I believe our time is now if we look around life as we know it is becoming exceedingly difficult to live in. I believe because we are so far out of order how GOD instructed for us to live hopefully before it is all said in done, we will live as one under GOD and his authority *AMEN.*

PEACE LOVE AND FAITH

Malcolm & Martin

Let us talk about two great leaders who had a lot in common first and foremost they both was two black men they both were married. They both fought for our civil rights they both had the same fight for justice they just went about it in a different way. These two men was both strong believers in their religions they both was two high profile men. These two black great men was well respected by the African American communities you know what else they had in common they both was shot and killed in the 60s.

The sad part about the whole thing is they did not work together can you imagine if they both were side by side daily. Marching the streets showing up together to fighting against injustice that was happening to black people hearing them speaking on the same mic to the same crowd. Malcolm than Martin or Martin than Malcolm how powerful that would have been.

The government loved the separation between the two black men they loved that one was Muslim and the other one was a Christian. Malcolm argues for black people to protect their selves against aggressive racist white people who was committing evil and violent acts against African American people.

Malcolm believed in standing your ground we are tired, and we are fed up the only way to stop a bully is to hit a bully back that was Malcolm and his Muslims brothers mentally.

With Malcolm being the strong minister that he was he wanted black people to stop fearing the same people who have what we have. Two arms two legs and feet two eyes two ears and one mouth and one nose to breathe through only difference between the people is skin color.

Living in A Country Influenced By Hate

Malcolm was very smart and highly intelligent that is what give him the edge over them in most of his interviews they could never pick him apart. Many of times Malcolm reverses the question on them picking their brain. FBI said he was the most followed person in his time that tell you he was POWERFUL.

I can only imagine what it would have been like to see such encouraging, inspiring, inspirational, black men working together. Truly I believe they would have been a force to be reckoned Malcolm X was the true meaning of a man's man. Malcolm voice could get anyone attention draw you in the force behind it made you wanted listen to what he was speaking about.

Malcolm X you are deeply missed what you saw when you visited that religion country, I believe you are a part of the reason for many Muslims living in the United States today.

Martin Luther King I could say so many great thinking about this man, but I choose to say a selective few. First and foremost, this great man helped me to believe in change he helped me to have faith he helped me to be encourage. I remember as child how my school would show us a video of him speaking and preaching and his voice caught My attention.

Living in A Country Influenced By Hate

Mr. King believed in the word of GOD he believed in GOD'S miracles he believed fighting violence with violence would only bring more violence. King march through the streets of the south with the passion for freedom at a young age the African American community elected him to be there leader. This 25-year-old young man put a weight on his shoulder like he was 45 years old and this country we call America hated him.

America arrested this man every chance they could all because he would not back down from their hatred ways. Marching in a nonviolent way was something they just could not understand. King won the Nobel prize because his style of reaction was different from what they wanted it to be. King gave the black Communities hope through *CHRIST* if you go back and watch him king did it just like *CHRIST.*

King walked the streets without violence the same as *CHRIST* did king teach his congregation as *CHRIST* teach his disciples. After every march King would speak to the people as did *CHRIST* when he arrived at every city. Kings resemble *CHRIST* in many ways and no I am not comparing king to *CHRIST* I am only showing you how he stays obedient to our LORD.

Living in A Country Influenced By Hate

King showed the African American communities that we can get positive results through positive protesting using our mind as the muscle.

King taught us living in this time today bravely is more than throwing your hands back at someone who threw their hands at you first. Regardless who talked bad about him regardless who turned on him towards the end. King stayed true to his way and because of that we have overcame a lot, but we still have so far to go. Racism, black on black crime, hatred, the lack of Knowledge and opportunity a lot of these things we are doing to ourselves. If anything, I said about these two **GREAT BLACK MEN** are inaccurate please forgive me as a writer a black writer I needed to speak on them from my point of view. Especially writing a book about the injustice the black communities have to idea with I try to speak equally about both men. I do not believe one is better than the other I honor both men as my mentors thank you Malcolm X for your boldness and strong voice. Thank you, Martin Luther King, for not giving up but and kept pushing forward.

MARTIN & MALCOLM

Living in A Country Influenced By Hate

FEBRUARY 21st, 1965 MALCOLM

April 4th, 1968 KING

REST-WELL Our Mentors

Rest well our KINGS we have not seen any type of men black or any other color like you two was since your deaths. You give me reason to speak

Living in A Country Influenced By
Hate

on the streets of Philadelphia Pa you give me reason to fight for justice between the both of you we were blessed to have you. I may have not walked the walk with you I may not have taken a beating with you or I did not get arrested with you. Truly I wish I did the people who did was fortunate to have you. The 60s we had the civil rights movement, the Vietnam war, and three assassination of three great men one who was the president John F. Kennedy Thank you, Malcolm X, and Thank you Martin Luther King Jr. Your services to this earth and to our black Communities are well Appreciate it REST-WELL. REST-WELL John Lewis

Living in A Country Influenced By Hate

POWER TO THE PEOPLE A NATION UNDER GOD AUTHORITY 🏛️🏛️

SCRIPTURE 2 Timothy 3:1-5

Living in A Country Influenced By Hate

This scripture tells us exactly what we are experiencing right now in today's, society it is telling us these things needs to play out in -order to restore order destruction is the only way to rebuild.

End of Days

2 Timothy 3:1-5

But understand this, that in the last days there will come times of difficulty. For people will be lovers of self, lovers of money, proud, arrogant, abusive, disobedient to their parents, ungrateful, unholy, heartless, unappeasable, slanderous, without self-control, brutal, not loving good, treacherous, reckless, swollen with conceit, lovers of pleasure rather than lovers of GOD, having the appearance of godliness, but denying it's power.

Wow how accurate is this living in 2020 we see everything the scriptures have spoken of there will be difficult time look at Covid-19 over 150,000 people have die from this virus. This is something that was written over 2,000 years ago the vision GOD gave them about the future which is our present because of what was going on in their time.

Living in A Country Influenced By Hate

Lovers of self and lovers of money tell me we are not living in a selfish time. Everything is I need to get to a bag and mind my business. People really don't" care about it unless if it's concerning them or affecting them, the things people will do to get money. Kill, steal, and destroy anything in their path. Look how people substitute confident now of days with arrogant which give them such an ignorant attitude allowing them to be so abusive.

Having no respect for ourselves or for our parents now of days parents don't" respect their own children. Drinking and smoking weed, dippers, popping pills having sex with different people all in the view of their children eyes. This why we cannot break the chains because the things GOD gave us to live off and to live by, we are so ungrateful for them. Our wants always overpower our needs our fears always stand out more than our faith living unholy is way funnier than living for GOD.

People souls are very cold look how kids and women are being trafficking sold across the world murder rates in every state are at an all-time high. The devil goes after the heart because he knows GOD analyze the heart to see how pour it is so if he can turn one heartless it is a win for him and a sin for you. Once the devil controls the heart, we lose self-control and now we are out of control working to please the devil and becoming reckless.

Living in A Country Influenced By Hate

We are living in a world that are lovers of pleasure lusting off everything that is not of GOD because we know if sin is in it, GOD is not in it. Treacherous betrayal and deception are all in the same line as being disobedient I ask myself why is this?

2nd Timothy 3:1-5

Tells us to avoid such people because their negative energy is very influencing and if we are not living by faith our sight will catch their attention very easily.

It is extremely hard to avoid such people in this day and time because some will have the appearance of godliness but denying its power if we do not know GOD, we will be fool.

There is a spiritual war going on in the air and we must decide on which way we are going to go. I do not know what other religion books say but I do know what the **BIBLE** said I am quite sure other religion books speaks on the ending days.

I try to break this scripture down the best way as I see it if you disagree your opinion is well understood ending times are here. Get prepared and get right with **GOD** accept **CHRIST AS YOUR LORD AND SAVIOR** repent and ask for forgiveness. Become a new creature and start new from here on out Amen.

Living in A Country Influenced By Hate
Men Do HELP Men

Living in A Country Influenced By
Hate
Men Do HELP Men

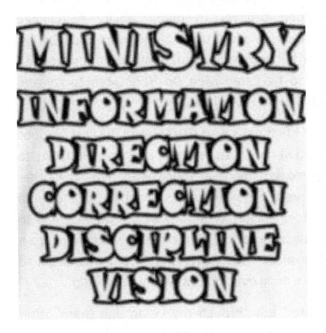

Understanding

Living in A Country Influenced By Hate
Men Do HELP Men

If you follow me and have read all three of my previous books you will know that I try to influence men and young teenagers' boys in every book. I am a strong believer in men's ability to change situations. A young man's mentor should be his father but sometimes situations may interfere with that, so I created **Men Do HELP Men** to try and fulfill that mentor place.

When I first got saved **GOD** placed different groups of men in my life to help me, one was SPIRITUAL to help me get more in touch with him. The other ones were physically and financially to show me how to manage my money and show me how to live in a legal society. Remember I was coming from a dark place where everything I did was illegal so transforming overtook some time and help.

I created this through my vision and many other great men vision watching them work with me and other men and boys gave me this idea. If we can get to the seed when it is blossoming meaning a young boy growing into a teenager, the impact can be significant. We see the effects the entertainment industry and the streets have on them because of what they see and hear so why not let them hear us.

Some way somehow, we must compete

Living in A Country Influenced By Hate

I believe if young boys and men add these seven words into their daily lives a change is possible for grown men transforming from negative to positive. Young boys possibly not even go the negative route

Correction

Direction

Discipline

Information

Vision

Understanding

Ministry

Put these words in whatever order best fit you if you read my second book ***One Man Journey Is The Next Man Path*** you will see how I broken the words down to fit into my lifestyle. These words brought me to where I am at in my life today, transforming my thinking came with each one of these words. Changing and remain change came with each one of these words. Now I know what may have worked for me just might not work for you but try it.

Living in A Country Influenced By Hate

I am living proof these words added into your life can work all I am asking is give it a chance why not allow **GOD** to help you.

Ministry

When you hear ministry first thing you think is church or religion which is a part of ministry, we will get into that a little later in this paragraph. When I say ministry, I am talking about building a relationship with **GOD** first and foremost get to feel his presence in your heart.

Surrendered to his ways and allowed him to lead you on your path go to sleep every night with a **PRAYER** of thanks. **GOD WILLING** wake up the next morning with another **PRAYER** of Thanks. Gratitude will carry you along way you will become more and more encourage to want to get know **GOD** your **FAITH** in him will make you more of a believer.

As you keep moving forward you will recognize the shifting that is happening around you everything about you will change mentally physically and spiritually.

After all of this you will want to feel his presence a little bit more it could be on a Friday a Saturday or Sunday morning, afternoon, or evening it will be where **GOD** send you at. You see when I say ministry it is your relationship with **GOD,** I speaks on mine because I was led to **CHRIST** where I believe we all should be at. Nevertheless, **Men Do HELP Men** is not about leading you to religion that is your choice we just give the information to have helped you.

Understanding

Understanding plays the biggest role among these seven words the reason why I am saying this because without understanding you will not know what is going on. While I was building relationship with **GOD,** I ask him to give me understanding on what my purpose is and how do I go about it.

After I surrendered my life over to him, I did not know a thing I did not know which way to go yelling out **GOD SHOW ME THE WAY** please give me understanding of my new walk. I was so confused at first because I was not hearing anything back from him. Then as time went on things started to click for me, I started recognizing the tools he surrounded me with.

I started learning to work with my needs my thinking ability felted like it had enhanced to a whole another level not on an education level but on a more I know where **GOD** need me to go level.

Once you become aware of this word and understand the meaning of this word the role it will

Living in A Country Influenced By Hate

plays into your lifestyle after that it is skies the limits. I lie to you not I am only going off experience I walked this walk matter of fact I am still walking this walk anything that you do always get Understanding first.

Discipline

This is where your journey will become hard because now you will need to do some things you are not using to doing.

Just because you surrendered do not mean life will become any easier training yourself to do the right things is a battle. This is where that saying comes in it is hard to teach an old dog new tricks. Remember this you already have something good going your way **GOD** renewed your mind when he gave you understanding you must discipline your actions. Staying focus and distancing yourself from any distractions that will knock you backwards trust me this will be a struggle, and this takes time getting use too.

Once you master this strategy the rest of these words will fall right into line because now you have disciplined your heart with prayer, you're thinking and vision are discipline with your faith which will allow your actions to do what is needed for you.

Living in A Country Influenced By Hate

Exercising, eating healthy, managing your finances reading more all fall under the same umbrella you will see the difference within yourself.

Discipline changes things this new person you have become is going to appreciate your efforts on not giving up your reward will be worth the change.

Correction

Correction comes with growth you need to understand you cannot change anything from your past but, you can direct your present. Yes, you may ask those who you have wronged in your past for forgiveness some may forgive you and some may not. Correction means going forward and not backwards trying not to make the same mistakes will become your purpose.

Looking back over your past will help you in many ways to more forward fixing relationships with family members, friends, and the one you love.

Correction comes with discipline and understanding it also comes with rejection and disappointment just because you are trying to rewrite your wrongs everyone is not going to see your rights.

You will need to remain focus because a rejection could turn into a distraction which could lead you to go backwards. Therefore, I say this word correction is important because everything moving forward is your new beginning remember what your old life did to you. This new you are what you are living for never get offended if someone is trying to correct you. Learn the difference between someone judging you and someone asking you to correct something you did that may harm you.

Direction

You must know where you are going if you want to reach your destination because if you are just traveling with not since of direction you are heading for a dead end. The good thing you have going for you remember you surrender to **GOD** and asked him to lead the way on your new journey.

Direction is important yes **GOD** may be leading the way, but it is up to you to follow him where he is trying to take you. People will try to interfere and tell you to take a shortcut because this way is much easier and faster. Your journey will have many speed bumps in the road we know what speed bumps are designed for to slow you down if you start to get inpatient and go to fast.

Frustration will become a big part on your new journey sometimes it may seem like you are never going to reach your goal you have set. Things can become easily influenced but, once again you must remain focused **GOD** part is already done the doors are already unlocked.

GOD will never lead you on a dark path know your way because there is light at the end of the tunnel, I am a true witness to his signs, miracles, and wonders. Direct your path there is order in yours steps many will come behind you become the light they will need to see in their darkness.

Vision

This is not just about eyesight or what you can see in front of you vision is something that is planned out for you to achieve.

Goal settings are what you will need to do envision yourself reaching the highest elements possible first thing first you will have to start small than work your way up. Vision yourself taking your first step towards your goal than vision yourself completing it or completing them, because you will set more than one goal.

Like I said before vision is something you plan, it takes time and patience with a whole lot of hard work. Disciplining your actions to be consistent the level of effort you will need to put into reaching your potential will be all up to you. Remember that saying if you dream it you can achieve it never

Living in A Country Influenced By Hate

doubt yourself or what **GOD** has for you **GOD** will never bring you this far to turn away from you.

Your vision will only be as strong as you make it out to be do not get me wrong it is nothing wrong with being a dreamer. A dreamer is where you will need to start at, but a completer is where you will want to finish at. You are in control of your own destiny I know you will accomplish your goals everything you see yourself doing you will be able to do it. Your efforts will need to be bigger than your dream.

Information

This word information holds a lot of weight you will need this word if you are looking to achieve your goals do not just go off someone else's accomplishments. This is when you will need to surround yourself around a good group of people put your pride to the side and asked questions a close mouth does not get fed.

This is the part we do not like about success the reading, the searching, the asking, the studying, it could be out of a book or studying someone moves and ways. We get disappointed so many times when we see someone else's success but when we try and do the same thing the result might be different. Most of the time we jump into something headfirst without a clue for example just

Living in A Country Influenced By
Hate

because you worked as a waitress in a restaurant does not mean you are ready to become a restaurant owner tomorrow.

Do your homework and remember information is apart of making the necessary decisions to make the right corrections. *GOD* gave us understanding and wisdom the discipline you inherent will help you get to where *GOD* wants to take you to.

The *BIBLE* tells us to seek and you will find the lack of knowledge will be the reason my people will be destroy. Have patience and do the necessary research time will tell.

Men Do Help Men

Founded in 2015

Living in A Country Influenced By Hate

Founder

Marlon Reid

Hanging Is Still Going on In America in 2020

What is going on in America three Africa Americans males one Latin male and one African American

Living in A Country Influenced By Hate

black female all founded hung this summer. In every police investigation each one of these incidents police calling them a suicide. All these hanging was right after George Floyd death which was committed by a white police officer.

This does not seem strange we have not seen anything like this since the 60s this have lynching by a racist written all over it. Hey, I could be wrong but, four blacks and one Latin with everything going on in America today it is hard for me not to believe it.

One of the men found hung I read his family believed he committed suicide I cannot speak on his death what about the other four this is no coincidence. Read between the lines the civil rights movement are being re-enacted from the 60s. police brutality, hatred. Looking at the president of the United States saying whatever he wants to say he give them the fuel they need to enhance their fire

America is a country full of hate always has been look at the history behind the land of the free how could this country be called that when we were slaves to them for over four hundred years.

Living in A Country Influenced By Hate

What do we call this hanging, or do we call this lynching we know its murder committed by a rope, but they want us to believe this was suicide?

I am not going to believe that I do not care what their evidence says if they cannot produce a video showing me, they hung their selves I am not convinced. The only one I will consider the man who family said he is suicidal no argument there they know him best.

Good people the reason why I am speaking on this situation because this need to have light shined on it even if it was suicide than we need to take and either harder look at it. Now the investigation needs to be what led up to this and why?

My prayers go out to the families I am praying for healing, strength, and a peaceful heart. If you believe I crossed the line in anyway, please forgive me that is not my intention. My intention is to bring awareness to the people being though I am a writer this is what I do I speak on it from my point of view. This gives me the opportunity to voice my opinions about what is going on around the world.

Violence

This have been a brutal summer for the violence happening in our black communities' children have been the latest victims in this black on black crime.

Living in A Country Influenced By Hate

Pregnant women also have become victims this generation really do not care about taking a person life no love in these streets. Almost every single day there is a funeral going on in Philadelphia three hundred and sixty-five days in a year and I am talking about at least three and fifty days a funeral is going on. That means 350 people are dead meaning 300 of them was murder this is a pandemic. This should have every resident in Philadelphia matter of fact every resident in every state marching and protesting in the streets. America made violence cool through entertainment movies, TV shows, and music, which influences the black communities because black people are the entertainers. With the entertainment industry being so popular we the people really have a big task ahead of us this is going to take a nation under **GOD** working together to try and save our youth. Prayer and courage will be needed throughout this process victory will be won when it is all said and done. I give thanks to all the leaders in every city and state that are stepping up to the plate calling out for change to all the organizations that are putting together rallies and marching on the fourth front. *A CHANGE IS HERE.*

The reason why I wrote this book

There are many different reasons anger, courage, inspiration, justice, and because I am a writer and

Living in A Country Influenced By Hate

an author but, the main reason that sparked my interest to write this type of book was anger. Tired of the justice system the prosecutors, judges, jury, and most of all racists cops and racists people. The things they are constantly getting away with put a lot of rage inside of my heart no lie I started building up hate against all police officers. You can tell from the beginning of this book my writing habits had a lot of anger but as time went by, I settled down and calm down being an African American in this country could be unfairly.

So, you can see the reason why I tried to expose the so call good cops because they are the ones doing nothing protecting the bad ones and serving right next to them. When we are protesting the good cops are the ones on other side of the line pepper spraying and beating on us because we are marching for justice. You took an oath to serve and to protect the citizens meaning if your fellow officers are crooked you have a duty to do the right thing.

This is not about offending the police officers who stand by and do nothing this is to expose those who are empowered to do the right thing.

As I spoken on the laws of America you can see how I came after the so-called forefathers just

Living in A Country Influenced By Hate

thinking about slavery and what they have done to my ancestors.

Made me realize that I still feel some type of way about them and what they did to us, to me Lincoln may have signed the papers for our freedom but he did not do a thing to enforce it. A statue of Lincoln standing over a black man kneeling to him with his hand over his head is a disgrace. My attitude towards him I expressed it I, may be wrong about Lincoln but I have no apologies because that how I feel about him.

I talked about our constitutional right when the so-called forefathers wrote it, they did not write it for us as time went on, they decided to involve us into it. I could be wrong about that to, but this is how I see it because right now today they violate them whenever they want to.

So as you see I have the opportunity to share my thoughts with the world so I am taking advantage of it now here a picture of Lincoln statue you tell me if this not a disgrace or not.

Living in A Country Influenced By Hate

Now what do you think?

DISGRACE

Living in A Country Influenced By Hate

I am praying this book bring awareness and understanding to all people throughout the United States and around the world.

Me as an author I always try to encourage people and give them inspirational hope letting the world know that **GOD** is still in the **BLESSING** business. So, I talk about a ministry I started call **Men Do Help Men** giving so fundamental on how I came this far giving definition to a few strong words and how I applied them to my life. The vision is to open a building some day and try to have men working together to mentor the young in a positive direction.

Because of this black on black crime this building and ministry and organization are much needed my anger towards blacks killing blacks are at an all-time high level. If history proves to be right looked how the hands of black people killed Malcolm X I talked about how he was a force for us doing the civil rights movement. Our own race murder him just like what is going on today our own race murdering each other plain old sickening. I also talked about Martin Luther King an activist leader. A man who gave us hope that someday blacks and whites will be able to live together in peace but once again America showed their true colors and murdered him. I wrote about how I wish the two

Living in A Country Influenced By Hate

strong leaders had worked together how powerful of force that could have been.

Please do not get the wrong impression about me or this book I wrote a few things about the bad side of this country but in fact I am grateful to be living in this country we call the United States of America. This country gave me many opportunities despite of my skin color America still gave me a shot I just had to work at it a lot harder than the other race who lived here.

I do not want to discourage anyone who are living here already or anyone from another country that are trying to come here.

I just wanted to tell my story from my point of view about being an African American living in America the things we must deal with while living in this country. White people are not the only racists people living in this country racism not just towards people.

Living in A Country Influenced By Hate

PRAYER

Dear father **GOD** as I pray to you today, I ask that you give people the right understanding behind the words I have written in this book. I ask that you give the readers a open heart and mind a clear vision on the message I tried to bring. Father **GOD** thank you for each and every **BLESSINGS** for each and every opportunity you allow to come my way. I pray one day living in the flesh we will be able to declare **VICTORY IN JESUS NAME** over hate, drugs, violence, anything that has to do with sin. **Romans 3:23** for all have sinned and fall short of the glory of **GOD** but I know your grace and mercy give us reason to believe. Father **GOD** I know you are in control I question nothing I ask for forgiveness for myself and everybody living in this world. We shall overcome everything in **JESUS NAME AMEN.**

Living in A Country Influenced By Hate

Dedications

I would like to thank everyone for their support and their love you guys are the ones who allow me to keep writing. I appreciate the criticism I appreciate the cheers without you taking time out of your life to read about what I have wrote my last three books would not be possible. My first book **The Diary Of A Changed Man** had supposed to been my one and only book now look I am on my forth book. **Living in a country influenced by hate** a course **GOD** gets all the credit but you guys the readers get credit in the support department.

You guys are the greatest readers in this world you helped me to become a writer because of your support I believe that I can take this further than just writing books. A film is in the works **The Diary of One Man Journey** a YouTube web series are also in the works **Thank you**

Ps.

I dedicate this page to you guys the readers may GOD grant nothing less than peace, love, and joy MANY-BLESSINGS to all in JESUS NAME AMEN.

Living in A Country Influenced By Hate

Publishers notes

Written by author

Marlon Reid

Copyrights 2020 Marlon Reid

Library of Congress

Edited Services: *Marlon Reid Production*

Formatting Services: *Marlon Reid Production*

Cover Design Services: *Dynasty Visionary Design*

Published, Printer, Distributor: *Amazon*

A

Living in A Country Influenced By Hate

⬚Marlon Reid Production⬚

Living in A Country Influenced By Hate

Made in the USA
Middletown, DE
18 October 2020

22320078R00046